THE MONASTERY
OF THE HEART

THE MONASTERY
OF THE HEART

———— •◆• ————

*Benedictine Spirituality
for Contemporary Seekers*

JOAN CHITTISTER

BlueBridge

Published by
B l u e B r i d g e
An imprint of
United Tribes Media Inc.
Goldens Bridge, New York

www.bluebridgebooks.com

ISBN: 9781629190204

Cover design by Cynthia Dunne
Cover image: Pawel Opaska / Alamy Stock Photo
Text design by Cynthia Dunne

Printed in the United States of America
10 9 8 7 6 5 4 3 2 1

Contents

OUR SERVICE

OUR PROMISE

OUR SPIRITUAL GROWTH

Introduction

After more than fifty years of life in a monastery, I have begun to sift and sort the effects of it all, asking myself, what—if anything—of monastic life is worth passing on to others in this day and age? What of this life has any impact or import to populations other than monastic communities themselves—and how can those outside traditional monasteries, too, join throngs of monastics over the centuries who have found this life both enriching and enlightening?

This book is, then, a kind of guide and invitation for those seekers who stand in the midst of a seething, simmering world of spiritual as well as secular options, overwhelmed by choices, and looking for the rhythm of a better life. It suggests a model upon which to build—or rebuild—their own lives. It offers a template to guide them through the maze of empty promises, seductive dead ends, and useless panaceas the modern world, a spiritless culture, has to offer.

The search for God is an eternal one. It plagues every generation. It stalks every soul. It is the insistent, eternal cry for meaning, for answers to the questions, Why? And what? And for what purpose? It is the unending awareness that I am not alone in the universe, despite the fact that I do not know where I have come from or to what I'm going. It is the soulful pursuit launched to understand the Beginning of Life and to find the answer to its End. The search for God is the attempt to complete the incomplete in us. And it never stops eating away at the innards of our soul.

Every age, every path, has answered the questions of the spiritual dimensions of life in ways peculiar to itself, in language and symbols and lifestyles it could understand. For some, in the past, the search to unite with the One, with the Energy, with the Life of life, took the form of desert asceticism. For others, it lay in community and communal worship. For many, it was an attempt to withdraw from the business of this world in order to be better attuned to the next.

But for one man, for Benedict of Nursia, the spiritual life lay in simply living *this* life, our *daily* life, well. All of it. Every simple, single action of it. History attests to the proof of the power of such a life lived to turn the ordinary into an experience of the extraordinary union with the God of the Universe—here and now. Benedictine spirituality, the ongoing legacy of this sixth-century founder of cenobitic monasticism in the West, is proof of its enduring value.

This spirituality based on the Rule of Benedict, a communal lifestyle, is over 1,500 years old. It developed at a time when Europe lay in political, economic, communal, and social disarray. And it exists to this day—around the world. Anything that survives the ages with new vitality in every age is surely worthy of serious spiritual examination in our own.

Most significant, perhaps, is that instead of setting out to reform the decadence of sixth-century Italy, Benedict of Nursia simply ignored the cheap and chaotic superficiality of it all to live according to different standards, to walk a different path, to live the life everyone else lived—but differently. Through the ages, thousands of others have done the same. As a result, Benedictinism has evolved from age to age, until many different forms of its past impulses exist yet—but all of them as carriers of the original impulse.

Today, in this time of cataclysmic social upheavals, of global transitions, of technological breakthroughs of unimagined proportions, we must do the same. Old patterns are breaking down; and individuals, families, and small groups everywhere—in intentional communities and home worship, in parishes and prayer groups, through committed lifestyles and private disciplines—are seeking to shape new ways of living for themselves in the shell of the old.

This small guide—following the ancient Rule of Benedict that is still the basic worldview and organizational pattern for life in Benedictine monasteries everywhere—is meant to be a new way to live a meaningful spiritual life in the center of the world today, rather than withdraw from it. It does not abandon traditional Benedictine spirituality in favor of some new or exotic spiritual practice. On the contrary, it is anchored in the Rule, rooted in its values. It is an apple falling off an ancient tree, a cutting meant to grow steeped in its history, fresh in its form.

May the women and men, the families, the intentional communities who seek to create within themselves a Monastery of the Heart, find there the God who is forever seeking them.

OUR
SEARCH

1

A Seeker's Path

*"Your way of acting should be different from
the world's way."*

THE SEARCH FOR God is a very intimate enterprise.
It is at the core of every longing in the human
heart. It is the search for ultimate love, for total belonging, for the meaningful life. It is our attempt to live life
and find it worthwhile, to come to see the presence of
God under all the phantoms and shadows—beyond all
the illusions of life—and find it enough.

But the search depends, at least in part, on the complex of energies within us that we bring to the challenges of this seeking.

We do not all hear the same tones at the same vol-
ume, or see the same visions in the same colors, or seek

the same goods of life in the same way. The search for God depends, then, on choosing the spiritual path most suited to our own spiritual temper and character.

For some seekers, it is in withdrawal from society or by immersion in nature that God is most present. For others, the face of God shows most clearly in the face of the poor or is felt most keenly through the support of those with whom they share a common spiritual regimen. For many, it is a bit of both, a balance of community, contemplation, and commitment to the people of God. It is the search to belong to a group of fellow travelers who will hold us up when we fall, and urge us on to greater heights when we are afraid to strain for more. These are the seekers who are looking for others who seek what they seek, who care about what they care about, and who set out with them to make life richer and the world better than they could ever do alone.

But whatever the nature of a seeker's lifestyle, the search for God depends, as well, on the spiritual maturity it takes to move from one level of spiritual insight to another—rather than cling to the spiritual satisfaction that comes with earlier, less demanding, practices. The search for God depends on the desire to grow to full stature as a spiritual adult, to come to know the God who is as present in darkness as in light. It depends on the willingness to let God lead us through the deserts of a lifetime, along routes we would not go, into the Promised Land of our own lives.

Most of all, the search for God depends on fidelity to the demands of the search itself. It is the constancy of commitment which we bring to the spiritual path that prepares us to recognize and receive the fullness of it.

There is, as a result, more than one way to go about the journey to God.

We may seek God alone, in the silence of our own hearts, where our attention is centered in a keen and conscious way on developing an ear for the leavening penetration in our lives by the mind and Word of God. This is an extremely private and individual spirituality that emphasizes personal prayer and contemplation of the presence of God in life. But it is not the only way to God and, in fact, not the most common way.

Another kind of journey to God leads us to seek God with others in a covenantal common life, where by the physical joining of our lives together we become a daily witness to create in the world a community of strangers bound together by the will of God.

In our time, in a society that is both mobile and connected at the same time, there is still another possible way to make the journey to God—and that is in a Monastery of the Heart. Here we choose to seek God in step with others, even though not always in common with others—each of us on an apparently separate path and yet all of us in veritable community with one another on the way—as lifelines, as mentors, as guides, as models, as brothers and sisters in whose loving company we choose to make our common journey to God.

The Rule of Benedict recognizes the major differences among seekers' paths and alerts us as well to the subtle distinctions among them, so that we can begin our own spiritual journey both aware of the complex character of each separate lifestyle and prepared to bring ourselves to the way best suited to the enterprise for us.

In whichever of the lifestyles we find ourselves—the spiritually solitary of any stage of life, in covenantal communities of every size, or as individuals in a Monastery of the Heart, the networks of similarly committed individuals whose communal life is stable but not necessarily daily—we are on tried and true pathways to God.

We are all seekers of the God who is here but invisible to the blind eye; who calls to us but is unheard by those who do not listen; who touches our lives wherever we are but is unfelt by those whose hearts are closed to the presence of God—who is everywhere, in everyone, at all times.

When we seek to wed all three lifestyles in our own time, we seek to be in a Monastery of the Heart. Then our Rule is this one. Our spiritual guide is the Word of God. Our formative community is with those of one heart with whom we join on this way in a Monastery of the Heart—to find the God who emerges with inexorable fidelity in human form.

2

A Gentle Invitation

"Listen carefully to my instructions . . . With the good gifts which are in us, we must obey God."

THE PROLOGUE TO Benedict's Rule demands of us that we "Listen."

Listen to everything. Because everything in life is important. Listen with the heart: with feeling for the other, with feeling for the Word, with feeling for the God who feels for us.

Listen to the Word of God, the Rule says, "and faithfully put it into practice." To seek God in a Monastery of the Heart, then, we must, first of all, read the scriptures intensely. It is in the scriptures that the eternal vitality of Benedictine spirituality lies. It is through immersion in the Word of God that the search for meaning erupts into a life lived in union with the God whose presence we seek. As monastics of the heart we must read the scriptures day in and day out, till they ring in our ears, and fill our hearts, and become the very breath we breathe.

It is through the scriptures that we follow the Israelites and see at work in ourselves all that God saw in them: the worship of our private little idols of money and power and status that lure us away from the real treasures of life. We must, at the same time, come to trust that we carry within us the same signs of goodness and faith and desire for life that took Israel through the desert of despair to the Promised Land—and the opportunity to live a life dedicated to the will of God. We must come to see in them God's continuing patience and love for us, so that no amount of weakness in ourselves can ever discourage us from continuing on the Way.

We must follow Jesus from Galilee to Jerusalem, contending with the system, healing the people, doing good, excluding no one, being a voice for the voiceless, calling us all to follow him to the rising of the God-life in ourselves. We must put ourselves under the impulse of the Spirit and in the hands of the God who wills us well. We must give ourselves to the task of bringing about God's peaceable kingdom, wherever we are, in whatever we do.

We must "obey God," the Rule of Benedict says, "with the good gifts which are in us"—with all the good, all the love, all the talent, all the wisdom, all the care, all the concentration, all the abandon of soul that is in us. We must obey the voices of life that are being drowned out around us but are, nevertheless, heard by God always. These are the voices that call to us to obey the needs of the world, the cry of the poor.

They call us to the consciousness of the power of God's care for us, and the commitment to make that presence palpable in the world around us. There is no one in need within earshot of our hearts whom we may ignore—because in each of them is the living plea that we do the will of God. It is by helping those who cannot help themselves that we do our part in the co-creation of the world.

"Let us ask with the prophet," the Rule says, "'Who will dwell in your tent, O God; who will find rest upon your holy mountain?'" "Then, let us listen well," the Rule goes on, "to what God says in reply, for we are shown the way to God's tent. 'Those who walk without blemish and are just in all dealings; who speak truth from the heart and have not practiced deceit; who have not wronged another in any way.'"

The Benedictine heart echoes this cry for universal awareness. The very first word of this ancient Rule, "Listen," is God's constant and daily call to us.

It is a gentle, tender invitation, this call to create within ourselves a Monastery of the Heart. It is the call to go down deep into the self in order to find there the God who urges us to come out of ourselves—to do the work of God, to live in union with God in the world around us. It is not punitive, this call. It is not demanding, not harsh and unforgiving.

It is, instead, the daily guarantee that, if we will only begin the journey and stay the road—listening to the voice of God and responding to it with all our gifts and goodness—we will find that God stands waiting to sustain us, and support us, and fulfill us at every turn. God is calling us lovingly always, if we will only stop the noise within us long enough to hear.

In a Monastery of the Heart—in the riches of the tradition it offers and the treasures to which it leads, and in company with others who are seeking, too—find a loving spiritual guide to encourage your journey, to refresh your faith when life is dry and dark, when the days are long and draining, when you are inclined to forget that God is with us for the taking. Most of all, every day start over again.

Remember that life is for coming to see, one day at a time, what life and God are really all about. Life grows us more and more—but only if we wrestle daily with its ever-daily meaning for us. God is calling us to more than now—and God is waiting to bring us to it.

"Listen," the Rule says. "If you hear God's voice today, do not harden your hearts."

3

A Single Vision

"Perform the Opus Dei where you are . . . Those on a journey are not to omit the prescribed hours but to observe them as best they can."

THE BENEDICTINE RULE is based on the notion that community life is the preeminent form of the spiritual journey—because it provides for immersion in communal worship, private contemplation, shared wisdom, common ownership, and mutual service. But the Rule does not necessarily require community of place—the geographical confinement of all the members of one community to one location.

If and when distance made common sharing, common worship, the common life—with all its daily human contact and support—impossible, large monasteries, whose ministries and members were far-flung, have for centuries routinely organized the community into smaller units of a single system such as granges and missions.

What the Rule is intent on creating is a community of heart, a oneness of mind and soul, and a commonness of vision among the brothers and sisters that binds them in the common endeavor of commitment to an intense form of the spiritual life.

For the sake of the intimacy and bonding that a sense of real human community demands, the Rule asks two major things of us.

First, we are to be constant at prayer. We are to perform the work of God—pray the psalms and scripture—faithfully, wherever we are. We are to make prayer be the bond and constant source of inspiration and purpose and glue that holds us together, the touchstone of everything that has meaning to us. We are to pray by ourselves, if necessary, "as best we can," but in concert with the greater community, and together raise one voice to God.

Second, we are to live a single vision of life together, even though apart. We are to live Benedictine spirituality wherever we are, whatever we are doing. We are to care for those who commit themselves with us to create this new world within a world. We are to go the way together in heart and mind and soul and be there for the other as signs of the coming Reign of God.

To be "in the world but not of it" has always demanded an uneasy truce between the monastery and the society in which it blooms. We are not to take on the customs and the conversations, the values and the interests of a society whose heart is in another place than the one we nourish in our vision. But for the Benedictine heart, to which all things are sacred, the very act of making the crooked way straight and the desert blossom is itself a trust, one more reminder of the sacrament of ordinary life lived extraordinarily well.

The function of Benedictine life, with its community commitment, is *not* to hide from the world. It is to make community for others around it, to enable others to also draw from its well.

For a monastic to be anywhere in the world is meant to be simply another way of being present to what, and why, we say we are. Wherever we are, we are rooted in the spirituality of the Rule.

A Monastery of the Heart is our means now of taking what we have to where it is needed, beyond the geography of a monastery itself.

We join hands with those who, like us, are committed to stay on this path until it brings us—wiser and more seasoned than when we began—all the way to God, all the way home. The bearer of the monastic heart, either alone or with an intentional group, must radiate what is within to a wider world—and respond to it. Those who commit themselves to live by monastic values in a Monastery of the Heart must be bridges to a world without them, must be models and signs of another way to live. They must find their strength and their purpose by holding hands with those who join them on this way, so that no one can lose contact—not with the Benedictine tradition that has spawned them, not with the society in which they are embedded, not with one another— however far off the rest of the circle of seekers may seem.

To the monastic of the heart, community is not as simple as geographic location alone, however important, or good, or growthful the physical relationship among members is meant to be. More than that, community requires meaningful contact, a common vision, and the beating of a cosmic heart big enough to embrace all of life—as did Benedict himself when "he saw the whole world in a single ray of light."

OUR
INTERIOR LIFE

4

Prayer

"[Let us] lay our petitions before the God of all with
the utmost humility and sincere devotion."

BENEDICTINE SPIRITUALITY is rooted in the time-
lessness of scripture. But Benedictine spirituality is
not about the past. It is the story of God's way with the
world then, a model for our own responses to life now.
Benedictine prayer, the heartbeat of Benedictine spirituality, is always about the presence of God in time—this
time, our time, my time.

Benedictine prayer immerses us in the mind of God
for the world. We are confronted there with what living
the God-life requires of us if we are to be faithful all our
days. We are brought there to confront ourselves, as well.

It's in the here and now that the song of the psalmist,

the cry of the prophet, the call of Jesus, the wail of the human heart for its eternal home, all resound. And they touch us, too. They beckon us in our time beyond the emptiness of our own momentary desires to the eternal fullness that is God. By echoing the struggles of life, the challenges of every age, prayer immerses us in the fullness of the scriptures and their history of salvation. Most of all, it requires our own responses to life.

And yet, at the same time, prayer lightens the load which the works of the day deepen. We, like the generations before us, can see the works of God through the ages and take heart. The soul that is dry and dulled by years of trying to create a world that never completely comes, is restored in hope. Our hearts are healed of the wounds of the day. We are reminded daily in prayer of who we want to be at the deepest, truest part of us. And in prayer comes fresh direction and new energy to urge us on. It fixes the eye of the soul on the real ends of life when the daily goals of real time seem unattainable.

But most of all, perhaps, the daily cascade of prayer flows inexorably and feeds the streams of silence and sacred reading, public and private prayer, that are the pulse of Benedictine life. It is in this net of spiritual support that we are held up and carried on from one day to the next, sure of our purpose, certain of its end.

Clearly, it is not the sum of the prayers we pray that counts. Prayer, Benedict says, should be "short and pure." It is the way our prayer life changes our own hearts and lives—the way it makes us more centered in God, the way it makes us more aware of our own limitations—that determines its quality.

As regular as the movement of the clock, Benedictine prayer becomes for us the pulse of the day, the rhythm of a life that might otherwise be caught in the drumbeat of ambition or profit or self-centeredness. It is the sustaining force of a Monastery of the Heart in a demanding world. The psalms ply us with a universal memory of the universally poor and oppressed.

If we lose sight in the heat of the day of the call to co-creation, Benedictine prayer fixes us on the life of Jesus, who went from place to place doing good. When we would despair of ever winning the match against poverty, injustice, inequality, and exclusion, there in prayer is the sight of Jesus healing the sick, raising the dead, teaching women as well as men, and contending with the forces of oppression everywhere.

Prayer is the conversion of the self-centered self to the conscious contemplative, to the prophetic witness of the radical spiritual life.

Prayer in the Benedictine tradition, and so in a Monastery of the Heart, is said in concert with monastics of the heart everywhere, with those for whom care for the soul and care for the world are always equal concerns. Everywhere it springs from the reflection and soul-wrestling that brings us to the bar of our deepest selves, seeking forgiveness, pleading for strength. It is the sight of seekers everywhere—all of them, one inch at a time, co-creating a new world alone but together—that holds us up and carries us on when going on has become the most difficult task.

In a Monastery of the Heart, we do not pray merely to pray. We pray to become more of a sign of the mind of God today than we were yesterday. The Benedictine prays to put on the mind of God more and more and forever more. The daily dinning of the Word of God into the soul of the seeker changes both the seeker and the world in which the seeker plants the Word.

There is in the Benedictine spirituality of prayer, then, as much a consciousness of content as there is a choice of prayer forms and formats.

In thirteen chapters on prayer, the ancient Rule, in its specification of the psalms for the day, lays out the concepts upon which Benedictine spirituality rests: that good overcomes evil, that God is our strength, that God is present in every part of life, that God is our refuge, that God is merciful, that sin is destructive of both the self and the world, and that praise of God is the purpose of life.

In those ideas and that consciousness we rest, secure in the presence of God, certain of the love of God, convinced that our trust in God is never, ever in vain.

5

Silence

*"Monastics should diligently cultivate silence
at all times."*

S ILENCE IS THE mother of the Spirit. It births in us the
cloister of the heart. It brings us beyond the noise of
chaos and clutter and confusion of a spinning world to
the cool, calm center of the spiritual self.

Silence enables us to rest in that center, to allow God
to work in us there, to clear from our hearts whatever
thoughts or pain, desires or demands, clamor within us
for puerile attention—and so take us away from our
best selves.

In silence, we learn to listen to others who are also
seeking God. We are free enough now of the self-
centered self in us to hear the pain and the wisdom of

others. We can hear in them the truths they, too, have learned.

In the shadow of the wisdom of the world around us, our own wisdom may be midwifed into the light. Under the guidance of insights beyond our own, we come to recognize the questions we might never know existed otherwise. And if we listen hard enough, with an open heart, the wisdom of the other may launch in us the kind of spirited development that is broader than the boundaries in which we have been formed.

"It is written," the Rule teaches, "'In a flood of words you will not avoid sin.'" It is silence that keeps us from giving full rein to the empty imaginings and cruel commentaries always too fresh at hand in our narcissistic selves.

We are expected, invited, then, to surrender the satisfaction of the too sharp retort, the too sour remark, the too common temptation to dishonesty that comes with the rattle of empty speech, of speech that is not reflective, of speech that wastes the depth of life on the mundane.

In a Monastery of the Heart, we are challenged to exchange all those empty ideas for the depth of reflection, the calm of thought, and clarity of insight that silence brings in its wake to the soul that longs—in silence—for it to come. It's there that we are protected from our noisy selves and prepared for the work of God in us. In silence, we come to understand ourselves. We become able to hear the voice of God calling us beyond ourselves—always to the better, always to the more.

It is of the essence, then, that in a Monastery of the Heart space for silence be treasured and guarded, sought and made sacred so that the spiritual life will grow and flourish in us. Otherwise, in clatter and shallowness, only the weeds of empty words grow down into the soul and take root.

When we make space for silence in our lives, we give ourselves space to heal what it is in us that still simmers and burns—hidden away, sometimes even from ourselves, but fierce in its perdurance and its ability to scorch our souls. This ability of the ashes of time to smother our souls with the dead dust of events long past deadens the soul to the fire of new life. If only we would nourish it.

As the Rule reminds us, "It is written, 'The tongue holds the key to life and death.'" It is silence that shields us from our first impulses to resist changes or reject new challenges or rebut new ideas or denounce the ideas of others. The grace of silence saves us from ourselves. It refuses to let us use humor to wound, or sarcasm to degrade, or criticism to demean. "We absolutely condemn," the Rule teaches, "any vulgarity and gossip and talk leading to laughter."

Instead, silence lays us open to possibilities, to people, to ideas we would have otherwise forever scorned. Benedictine spirituality is embedded in both quiet and encounter, in contemplation and community. It is silence that is the circuit between the two. It is silence that prepares us to hear God.

It is also silence that makes fruitful the encounters we are meant to serve in the spirit of God. For speech not tinged by silence, the Rule teaches, "we do not permit a disciple to engage in words of that kind."

Regular periods of solitude and silence, then, comfort, heal, and restore us to ourselves—fresh and new and quieted. Silence prepares us for prayer. It gives us new energy for life. It takes us to the depth of the soul and the mountaintop of life to stretch our vision and rest our souls for the journey to God that never ends.

The noise outside of us is not the enemy. It is the noise within—our desires that plague us, our worries that deplete us, our thoughts that agitate us—that we must calm.

It is the noise within which life in a Monastery of the Heart enables us to transcend and to transform. Out of that chasm of silence the soul rises to commune with the rest of creation—and in that process walks into the heart of God.

6

Prayerful Reading

"Listen readily to holy reading."

BENEDICTINE SPIRITUALITY is not an exercise in private devotion or personal pieties. Benedictine prayer is not simply ceaseless recitation of scripture passages and psalmic verse. It is the beginning of a lifelong conversation with God.

To deepen that conversation, to give it flow and substance, meaning and heart, the Benedictine is to read the scriptures and holy books, reflect on them deeply, and respond to them consciously and personally. Then, at long last, after years of softening the soil of our hearts with the Word of God, we come to radiate the meaning of it for all the world to see.

So important is this process in Benedict's view that he legislates the hours of the day in which sacred, prayerful reading—lectio—is to take place. "They will devote themselves to their reading," he says, and allows no other activity to interfere with it. No other activity at all.

In one of the most telling elements of the Rule, Benedict inserts a consideration of lectio in what might seem today—when reading is a popular pastime—a very strange place. It is in the chapter on "The Daily Manual Labor" where he talks most directly about the place of reading and reflection in Benedictine life. Reading, it seems, can be one of the most important spiritual works of the soul.

Lectio, this unplumbed, personal response to the cycles of prayers and readings that make up the Liturgy of the Hours—the daily choral prayer common to traditional monastic life everywhere—is to be taken seriously. As seriously as any or even most other practices of the spiritual life. Reading is, in fact, to be worked at.

Nothing is left to chance here.

In Benedict's time, in a culture more illiterate than not, in communities of peasants and craftsmen, shepherds and men-at-arms, he required the work of the mind. He placed constant and unconcealed emphasis on the harrowing of the soul with the ideas and sacred stories and the words of the holy ones who went before.

Benedict wants us to reflect on ideas, not simply to

collect them or repeat them or accept them unknow-
ingly. Ignorance, he knows, enslaves the soul in a regimen of substanceless devotions. It limits our insights into
the expansiveness of a cosmic God. Any limitation on
thought and reflection reduces the spiritual life to a kind
of pietism that is unworthy of the life-changing profun-
dity of the Gospels.

In a Monastery of the Heart, it is lectio, prayerful
reading—my personal reflections on the words and
challenges of scripture, on the eruptions of nature, the
vagaries of life, the insights of poets and artists and holy
teachers—that really stretch my soul.

It is these words that confront my daily life with the
daily face of God. They stir my heart with the words of
Jesus. They bring me heart-to-heart with the psalmist's
cry of universal pain.

Lectio is the bridge to a mature spirituality. Reflection, the soul's wrestling match with God, demands my
personal response. It refuses to allow me to ignore the
continuing cries of the God who pursues me in the
ordinary circumstances of life, day after day, hour after
hour, every moment of my life.

This careful prayerful reading is intense meditation
and reflection on one word, one sentence, one image,
one event, one idea at a time.

Lectio frees us from our misperceptions about Jesus
as a figure of love without purpose. We see with our
own heart now that Jesus is no doer of miracles without

meaning, no model of personal care for others without social concern for society as a whole. We see for ourselves now that it is this Jesus of the highways and byways, of the sinners and the sick, of heretical questions and curious disbelief who calls us to reexamine our own sense of what it means to be "spiritual."

It is lectio that gives the contemplative orientation to Benedictine spirituality in a Monastery of the Heart. It integrates practice and meaning.

At base, lectio makes the spiritual life more than a round of exercises. It makes it personal and mystical, vision-filled and prophetic.

The contemplative sees the world as God sees the world, because the contemplative spends life rooted in the kind of reading and reflection that breaks open the heart to the mind of God. A spiritual life without regular, daily, sacred reading and reflection lacks the pillars on which a lifetime of spiritual insight depends.

Lectio deepens the holy leisure of silence and solitude. It fills us with the substance we need if we are to make the spiritual life real. This steady drip, drip, drip of the call of Jesus to our world, the repetition of the urgent Word of God, and the persistent presence of the Spirit makes us doers—and not just hearers—of the Word.

Holy reading is the beginning of union with God here and now that brings serenity, courage, and meaning to everything else we do in life. It defines our purpose, it gives light to the way, it sparks courage in our hearts.

The nourishment of both mind and soul far beyond the routine of daily prayer comes only from lectio. It is the foundation of Benedictine spirituality. By opening us to the Word, it prods us all to grow beyond the pious rituals of present routine. It breaks us open to the fullness of an unknown future that is as much mystical as it is faithful to the daily contours of life in a Monastery of the Heart.

7

Retreat and Reflection

*"The life of a monastic ought to be
a continuous Lent."*

LIFE IS NOT lived in a straight line. We do things one day and regret them another. We make plans that never come true—and only realize later what there was about us that blocked our hopes in the first place. Life takes reflection. Sometimes repentance. Always repair.

There is a time in every life when the very act of looking back becomes essential to going forward. The difficult moment cannot be avoided any longer. It is time to take stock. Just myself and I—with no one around to impress, no one to whom I could explain away the real me. If anything in life is going to get better now, only truth-telling can show the way.

Without the light that shines out of the darkness of the past, we cannot chart a new path to the future. Which is why monastic spirituality is built around a life of retreat and reflection.

"The life of a monastic," Benedict writes, "ought to be a continuous Lent"—a life in which holy reading, self-control, and reflection on the great questions of life should be of the essence. Only understanding of the past taken seriously can help us change direction or even to continue a present that—however good it is—has lost its excitement, its flair.

Which is why, for those with a Benedictine heart, a Lenten spirit is *not* an exercise in spiritual athleticism designed to show that my fasting is better than your fasting. In a Monastery of the Heart, the Benedictine soul learns always to return to the cave of the heart, where the superfluities of life do not distract from the significance of life. What we need, Benedict knows, is the spiritual courage to cultivate a reflective soul and a disciplined mind that goes regularly into "retreat." We must go into that space where we look, first of all, at what we set out to be, and then look consciously at what we are now doing to get there.

Retreat time is the practice of making personal time for the kind of spiritual time that is beyond the routine of religious practices or spiritual duties.

Part of our spiritual journey, Benedict implies, must— if the soul is to make progress in the spiritual life—be spent remembering what we say are our intentions in life, in the light of what we can clearly see are becoming the patterns and actions of our lives.

In fact, even during Lent the Rule does not call the Benedictine to rigorous asceticism. What we're called to do is to pray more thoughtfully, to read more intensely, to feel more keenly the distance between who we say we are—and what we know ourselves to be.

Life in a Monastery of the Heart is meant to freshen the embers and stoke the fire of fidelity, to deepen our understanding of the great treasure we seek. It is designed to bring to new life in us again the sight of the road on which we have put our feet.

The monastic heart sets up a rhythm of life that moves seamlessly between contemplation and action, between work and Sabbath, between regular quiet and reflection times throughout the year.

The Rule's call to make life "a continuous Lent"— to reflect always on what we're doing and how we're doing it—is, then, Benedict's antidote to religious posturing. There is a temptation in religious life, the Gospels warn us, to play religious, to dress the part of the seeker, "to put on a gloomy face" in order to look wan and worn out from fasting. But what is more growthful, the Rule demonstrates, is to ask ourselves regularly about all the little ways we are tempted to cut the corners of the spiritual life: there is the notion that we don't really need formal prayer anymore, for instance. We can simply cease to pray, we tell ourselves. Or we can give up studying the insights of the saints who went before us. We can give up on living the faith by failing to grapple with the scriptures, by neglecting to go out of ourselves to meet the needs of others, by refusing to tell the world a Gospel truth, by forgetting to give voice to the pain of the world, by identifying with the ambitions of the profiteers instead of taking up the challenges of the prophets.

Times of personal reflection remind us always to make the space to begin—again—and, in the midst of the cloying demands of work and family, of money-making worries and the stressors of social systems, to fix the eye of the heart on the really important things of life.

In every Monastery of the Heart, there must be regular times set aside to go down into the inner recesses of the soul once more, alone and centered, to take another look, a new kind of look, at ourselves.

Retreat, reflection, Sabbath, and soul-space are of the essence of the monastic spirit—not for our sake alone but for the sake of those who depend on us to make the promise of creation new again.

First, painfully aware of our own lack of steeled spirit, and full of compunction—what the ancients called the regret of the soul—we must forgive ourselves for being less than we know we can be.

Second, we must turn the compass point of the heart

back again to where God waits for us, arms open, full of mercy, made of love, to be our own best selves—not for our own sake alone but for the sake of the rest of the world.

Benedictine spirituality, after all, is life lived to the hilt. It is a life of concentration on life's ordinary dimensions. It is an attempt to do the ordinary things of life extraordinarily well.

OUR
COMMUNITY

8

Mutuality

"We intend to establish a school for God's service.
We hope to set down nothing harsh,
nothing burdensome."

COMMUNITY IS a matter of the heart and the mind. No amount of space can guarantee it. No degree of separation can provide it. It is of the essence of the soul.

The people and ideas and places we identify with give us a home away from home. Wherever those ideas are honored and those places are welcoming, we know support. The goals that excite a sense of purpose in us make us a genuine part of a changing world; they give us both direction and community. The people and places that give us a feeling of belonging and support—it is those realities that create community for us.

In the Rule of Benedict, community is made up of common worship, common ownership, and common life. It is about having little or nothing of my own, on the one hand, and having a right to everything the community owns, on the other.

A community of mutuality is about drinking from the same well of belief and giving myself to the same life goals, and aims, and objectives as those with whom I have promised to make this journey.

But community cannot be accomplished without making some kind of connections. The problem is that in the modern world—where business outreach and networking are tools for success rather than bonds for life—connections alone are no guarantee that a real community will really form. "Connections" has become a code word for making "valuable"—translate: status-enhancing—associations. In this age, it means having a contact list of important phone numbers just in case we ever need friends in high places.

Community in a Monastery of the Heart cannot be accomplished without making some kind of connections—but connections alone are no guarantee that a real community will really form.

To become community in a Monastery of the Heart requires regular and meaningful interaction among the members. It is more than calendrical or routine celebrations, as important as these are, for the building of a common spirit.

A Monastery of the Heart requires the process of creating and sharing mutual bonds. It shares the faith life that underpins a group. It supports the personal life and affections of each member. It nurtures the emotional life that forms and fluctuates and drives each of us at different levels at different times. And most of all, it sets out to explore together the undercurrents and ideas and concepts that stir our attitudes and hopes for the human enterprise. It requires that we listen to one another, in the awareness that in listening lies learning. It means that we each draw from the same spiritual well and together set out to make it real in the here and now.

A community of mutuality always means that we're in this together. And if we're lucky it means that the group knows us well enough to be happy that we're there.

Community is the backdrop against which we do what we do. It gives us the solid foundation that enables us to go on when we're tired, to go forward when we're afraid, to go more deeply into the unmasking of the self when everything inside of us seems to have gone to stone. Gone dry and dull and lethargic.

Community building does not just happen. It cannot be taken for granted. It requires both great faith and great trust that is generated by a continuing display of great human care that begins with me, and then comes back to me. It takes a great deal of energy to create community. And in today's world, community takes many shapes.

The kind of community for which the ancient Rule of Benedict is written, is based on a great deal of common physical presence.

But as the world enlarges, so does the concept of community. The physical is still important—but differently. Now community is often virtual, but just as real in many dimensions as sitting next to the same person in chapel our entire lives.

In a Monastery of the Heart, what is important is that we each be an extension of the Gospel, and an extension of each other, and an extension of Benedictine spirituality at the same time. Wherever we are—alone or together.

What is imperative is that the sharing of the common mind be just as important as once was the sharing of a common schedule, or a common place, or a common work.

What is central is that together we use our goods for something greater than ourselves—that we "do not store up grain in barns," as the scriptures say, for our own security alone, but use the profits of our labor for the good of others, as well.

It is a process of making all of human community real, and of doing it out of a common vision and one heart, in whatever form is available—so that the spirit of community that is Benedictine to its core may spread like a holy spirit throughout the world.

9

Equality

*"Monastics keep their rank in the monastery
according to the date of their entry and the virtue
of their lives."*

WE LIKE TO THINK that equality is the basic char-
acteristic of this—our—period of history.

Ironically, *inequality* is the great sign of our time.

Today, everyone is supposed to be able to get ahead,
to have the same rights, to be equally protected under
the law, to have the same opportunities as everyone
else.

But it is also our world that enslaves the poor to the
drudgery of survival, that ranks women as lower human
beings than men, that distributes the goods we produce
according to race, that worships at the feet of the gods of

money and lives in gated communities in order to keep the rest of the world out.

To this world, Benedictine spirituality says clearly, "No." Not race, not age are the carriers of the Benedictine tradition. Not money, not class, not gender, not educational status determine the nature of a Benedictine community. There is no status here.

Authority comes and goes regularly in communities where responsibilities are shared and cyclical. In truth, authority is everywhere a movable feast. Sooner or later every office we achieve disappears. What is forever left in communities is simply ourselves, nothing more and nothing less.

We keep our rank in the monastery, the Rule says, based on the date of our entry and the virtue of our lives.

Those who are longer-lived, older in the life, who have borne the heat of the day longer, more intensely, more consistently, are the community's elders, its wisdom figures, its spiritual icons. These become signs to a growing community that, indeed, life grows sweeter with time, that life grows holier with experience, that life grows richer of heart as the heart grows deeper into God.

But age and seniority are also not its gods. The Rule writes, in accordance with the scripture, "Absolutely nowhere shall age automatically determine rank. Remember that Samuel and Daniel were still boys when they judged their elders."

Consequently, both in a Benedictine community and in a Monastery of the Heart, there is no ranking of people by any social criteria, regardless of the norms of any other organization around it.

Here we are all equal at the table—even when the direction of the community itself is at stake. "As often as anything important is to be done in the monastery," the Rule reads, "the prioress or abbot shall call the whole community together . . . the Spirit often reveals what is better to the younger."

The principle is a clear one: "The Spirit blows where it will." We cannot damp down the fire of the Spirit on the basis of anything but the greater movement of the Spirit itself. It is from this perspective that a Benedictine looks at the world and lives in it, and works in it, and plans for it. In the Benedictine heart no door is closed, no lines are drawn. No ideas are smothered before they have ever been examined in the light of day.

In a Monastery of the Heart, as well, whoever else makes enemies of differences, the seeker listens ever harder to learn what differences have to teach, what otherness has to say. Benedictine spirituality takes in difference and makes it its own. It is the learning tool of a healthy and developing community. It is an equality of the soul, a gift of common mind, a sign of what it means to have the heart of Jesus.

Equality is the very ground of mutual obedience. Neither age, nor race, nor sex is a valid measure of wisdom.

Benedictine communities, based on equality, deliver us from social bias and groundless prejudices.

As a result, a Monastery of the Heart must be based on mutual respect and grounded in mutual affection.

It is this that makes "community"—however it is formed, and meets, and prays together, and seeks the good as one.

It is "community" that makes the monastery as human as it is holy—and as holy as it is human.

Equality does not interrupt the presentation of ideas that members offer the group. It does not demean them or disparage them or mock them or deride them. It does not dismiss easily or idly the insights, the concerns, the questions or the answers of the other.

It does not build walls around the heart.

Equality, the offshoot of humility, sees in the face of the other—all others—the face of God.

Without it, no group, and no Monastery of the Heart, can ever be really sure that whatever it thinks it knows about the spiritual life, it really knows fully.

10

Spiritual Direction
and Counsel

*"Do everything with counsel and you will not
be sorry afterward."*

BENEDICTINE SPIRITUALITY sets out to build communities that, together, seek the universal God, hold the wounded of the world in one heart, and serve the world by being for it oases of peace and prayer, beacons of truth and justice.

To do this in a Monastery of the Heart—where coming to know one another intimately requires more than the routine of a daily schedule—community as a dimension of life takes distinct and regular effort. Community building is about more than effecting a communal design or even a desire. It is about being part of the glue that holds a wounded world together. It demands care and affection, understanding and support.

It requires that we explore and support the gifts of each and every person we meet in conscious and committed ways. In a very human, human community, we work together to release one another's gifts so that the communal voice can be stronger than any one of us can ever be alone.

To do that, the ideas of each person in the group must be both solicited and respected, the needs of each must be met, and the energies of all must be put in the service of the whole society. To do that, the community consciously binds itself together for the sake of learning from the wisdom of all.

But none of that can be done alone. All of that requires mutual support, the primal substance of a good and healthy community.

Clearly, then, Monasteries of the Heart, like all Benedictine communities of whatever structure and shape, are not loose confederations of independent individuals. Neither are they monarchies in which individuals, in the name of holiness, are expected to give up both their right to have their voices heard and their responsibility to speak their truths. On the contrary, those who seek community must do as much to create it as they do to find it. Only then will Monasteries of the Heart stir in us—and in others—a commitment to create a world more given to communal values than to self-serving individualism.

Most of all, to do these things we must be aware of our own need to go on growing. Life prods us unendingly to go on stretching ourselves to the boundless limits of the human soul. But that takes counsel, that takes spiritual direction, that takes our own willingness to learn from the wisdom and guidance of others, of those wise and holy souls who have themselves plumbed the depths and pain, the challenges and real victories of life.

It is, then, in choosing our counselors and identifying our spiritual directors that we each take our own soul in our hands.

It is easy to choose as counselors—experts, friends, authors, preachers, or spiritual directors—those who claim to have answers we do not want to trouble ourselves with discovering. Better to simply follow orders, we are tempted to believe, than to make the effort to participate in the hard, slow process of determining for ourselves, alone or together, what is the holiest of holy possibilities in the sight of God.

What is dishonest is to choose for guides those who allow us to drift into nice, comfortable, secure superficial practices that promise quick fixes for the lack of a genuine spiritual life. Such things may pass for holiness but, if truth were known, they do little more than mask a deep-down resistance to the process required for authentic spiritual life. There is a plethora of them.

The complacent seeker asks no difficult spiritual questions that might require new efforts to answer.

The comfortable pilgrim opens no new or challenging paths that might challenge the self-proclaimed gurus around her.

The self-satisfied spiritual pawn carves out no new directions, risks no new questions, that might disturb the soulless apathy that comes to anyone over time.

The placid enthusiast foregoes prophetic spirituality to live the God-life in the midst of the profane and chooses for himself guides who maintain the system in the spirit of the past, but do little or nothing to stretch it to the full height and breadth and depth of itself.

The Rule of Benedict is clear about the nature of the spiritual counselors for which we must look:

The authentic spiritual director is an example to the community of its best self: open, loving, hospitable; committed to the study of the Word; kind and understanding of the struggles we all face on the way to the holy emptiness of self that is full only of God.

The genuine spiritual director "must point out . . . all that is good and holy more by example than by words," the Rule teaches.

The great spiritual counselor values the Gospel more than public approval.

The holy model we choose must be committed to the needs and growth of the entire human community, be even-handed in their love for all people from all walks and facets of life, and, the Rule says, must "avoid all favoritism in the monastery."

The model in whose path we choose to walk must maintain the integrity of the spiritual life and encourage us to be what we are meant to be: a sign of the world to come, a bringer of peace, a haven for the homeless, the heart of God on the streets of the city, a light in the dark to those who seek peace and justice and human community.

Identifying and choosing good spiritual guides is of the essence of spiritual development. We become what we choose.

If we choose to be a Monastery of the Heart where love casts out fear, we must choose those as our spiritual guides who know how to embrace, with wisdom and truth, friend and stranger alike.

If we choose to be a justice-seeking Monastery of the Heart, we must choose those who are willing to risk themselves publicly for the sake of the Gospel.

If we choose to be a peace-making Monastery of the Heart, we must choose those who can find in differences the very breadth of God.

More, whatever the choices made around us, in a world of competing interests, we must always, as individuals, choose to follow those whose lives have been lived with love and justice, with open arms, and with hearts that beat for the poor.

Each member of a Monastery of the Heart must

bring their personal influence wherever they are—in the local community itself and through their presence in the world at large—to lead the way toward justice for the sake of the world.

We must seek our counsel and direction from those who forever put the God-life above everything else, including the systems in which they live.

And, most of all, we must be faithful to immersion in the Spirit and open to the presence of God in the mind and soul of the community.

11

Sufficiency
and Sharing

"Do everything with moderation."

THE PURPOSE OF the monastic life is never to amass
wealth for the sake of the self. Instead, Benedict's
definition of the relationship between persons and things
is sufficiency—not frugality. Benedictine poverty does
not reject the good things of life; it simply refuses to
amass them, to make things and money the center of life.

Benedictine spirituality does not see indigence, abject
poverty, stringency, and parsimoniousness as a lifestyle to
be desired, let alone a high-level signal of holiness.

The monastic ideal is about the ability to understand
the difference between need and want, and between

having what is necessary rather than doing without what is necessary, simply for the sake of doing without.

Those who follow the Benedictine way understand the personal impact and social import of what it means, in a starving world, to "hold all things in common."

In a world where the accumulation of goods, money, power, and property denies millions the basics of life—their wages, their resources, their education, their health, their future—Benedictine spirituality confronts that kind of engorgement with the principle of sufficiency.

"It is written," the Rule says, "Distribution was made as each had need." And, "Whoever needs less should thank God and not be distressed, but whoever needs more should feel humble because of their weakness . . ."

It is not the rejection of the goods required to make contemporary life manageable—cars, computers, electronics, phones—that is the measure of sufficiency for the Benedictine heart. It is the rejection of over-consumption, the unmitigated greed that drives a person to have, in undue measure, what others have little or nothing of—to want for the self rather than for humanity—that distinguishes Benedictine poverty.

Benedictine poverty does not require us to refuse to have money or earn a salary or support ourselves "as our ancestors did." On the contrary, it simply confines us to what is necessary—so that we can help to sustain those who cannot earn the money they need to take care of themselves.

In a world where the scales of wealth tip precipitously toward the West, the white, the male, and the few at the top everywhere, it is Benedictine spirituality that refuses to give in to the acquisitiveness and amassing of goods.

It's the delusion of having to have at our disposal ten kinds of potato chips, thirty pair of shoes, the biggest and best of everything, that, in the end, wars against the desire of the heart to live a simple but sufficient life.

In a Monastery of the Heart, seekers live with one eye on the needs of everyone else as well as their own.

When we find that we have accumulated good things in multiples and use few of them ever, it is time to give some of them away to those who have none.

It is not necessary to look poor to live a simple life. But it is necessary to love simplicity, to gather only what is necessary for ourselves, not necessarily to have the best, the most, the latest, or the most expensive, let alone to have all there is of anything.

To form a Monastery of the Heart in our time, the commitment to the development of Benedict's concept of community must be far wider in this century than it was in the sixth century. It must burst through every kind of monastery gate into a world where national laws and local prejudices fail to take into account the effects of our over-consumption of food, energy, resources, and weaponry on those who find themselves hungry, empty-handed, and sick.

In a Monastery of the Heart, we must begin to define

community globally rather than simply locally, and work at every level to make it so. We must see the moderation of consumption as our way to reach beyond the boundaries of our own lives to the obscenely poor—who stand outside looking in at our three-car garages and second homes and wish for simply enough of what we have to live a humanely human life themselves.

12

Nourishment

"Nothing is so inconsistent with the life of the
monastic as overindulgence."

THE SEEKER'S IDEAL is to be "in the world but not of it"—to be like everyone else but different where it counts.

For those who seek to define this *other* quality of life by the development of a Monastery of the Heart, the relationship between what it means to belong to both the world around us and the monastery is an especially important one.

How, for instance, shall we eat and drink as monastics of the heart in a world half-starving on one hand, and meant to be enjoyed on the other?

How does Benedictine spirituality define our attitude toward matters of the body?

Whatever its stress on communal welfare, the Rule of Benedict is very much attuned to individual differences. Nowhere is it clearer on that point than in the chapters on the proper amount of food and drink.

In an era still attuned to desert monks, with all their asceticism and strict dietary rules, the community lifestyle of Benedict of Nursia never approves of extreme asceticism—practices which are often a source of spiritual pride, and always a source of spiritual distraction.

Benedictinism understands that differences are the strength of every community—and the challenge.

"It is, therefore, with some uneasiness," Benedict says in the Rule, "that we specify the amount of food and drink for others." And he doesn't. Instead he legislates for choice and for personal comfort.

He warns against gluttony and drunkenness, but he allows wine, for instance, "with due regard for the infirmities of the sick," and requires that at least "two kinds of cooked food" be served at every meal, so that no one went hungry in a culture where monastics were expected to be abstemious.

"If fruit or fresh vegetables are available," the Rule continues, "a third dish may also be added." And except for the very sick, Benedict wants all to "abstain entirely from eating the meat of four-footed animals."

What are we to think of these guidelines in today's

culture of excess? Is it "religious," "holy," "spiritual" to be fed with care and trusted to know when enough is enough? Is it monastic to live on anything but bread and water?

The answer is a plain one in the context of the Rule: sanctity is not about excess of *any* kind, not the physical, not even the spiritual. It is about dealing with all the good things of life in moderation, properly, appropriately.

A study of human nature, and an awareness of the gift of the senses, makes the conclusion clear: restraint is just as holy as self-abnegation—maybe, in some instances, more so.

We do not become holy on food and drink—either the kind we eat and drink, or the kind we do not. Holiness is made of sterner stuff than that—however much great fasting may impress the world with our purported sanctity.

Benedict says, "We read that monastics should not drink wine at all, but since the monastics of our day cannot be convinced of this, let us at least agree to drink moderately, and not to the point of excess, for 'wine makes even the wise go astray.'"

It is not the wine, it is the "falling off"—the excess—that is the problem. It is the ability to set limits for ourselves—and to keep them. It is the ability to meet the standards of the highest level of human development that is the mark of the truly monastic soul.

Benedictine spirituality is a spirituality based on the

awareness that everyone—to work, to enjoy life, to concentrate on more than their appetites—needs the staples of life.

Benedictine communities in the Middle Ages made the fields flush with crops and taught peasants to farm so that everyone in the area—nobility, townspeople, and peasants—could all live without fear of starvation, could feed their children and sustain their families.

In our day and age, then—when joblessness and low wages, high costs and limited opportunities, plague families everywhere and on all levels—to be spiritual, the Rule warns us, we must be most concerned with those who do not have food and staples, and be just as committed as our ancestors in the faith to seeing that the hungry around us, too, are also fed.

In a Monastery of the Heart, we learn from the Rule and the tradition that what we enjoy for ourselves, we must supply for others, as well.

Benedictine spirituality does not depend on symbolic actions as the hallmark of its quality. It requires us to do every tangible thing we can to create a human community—as decent and as humanly dignified as our own.

OUR
SERVICE

———— •◆• ————

13

Good Work

"When they live by the labor of their hands, then they are really monastics."

PRAYER AND CONTEMPLATION, Benedict is clear, are no substitute for work. Nor are they an excuse to detach ourselves from the holy act of human responsibility for making the world go round.

The simple truth is that sloth is not a Benedictine virtue. Work, for the sake of hastening the coming of the Reign of God, is every bit as much a part of Benedictine life as prayer times and holy reading.

In fact, it is not just any work with which the Rule is concerned. It is "the daily manual labor," the work of the hands, the kind of work that makes things happen.

To avoid manual labor entirely is to participate in

the cultivation of a classist or racist or sexist society—in which some of us think they do the really significant things of life, and others of us do the physical work the rest of us think we are too important to do.

Whatever our motives might be, to absent ourselves from manual labor is to participate in the creation of a servant society in which we give ourselves the right not to serve.

But Benedictine spirituality is about equality and community, about service and mutual support. And that takes many forms, not simply one. The Benedictine heart knows that attending to the mechanical functions of what it means to get through a day—running the vacuum, washing the dishes, shoveling the snow, doing the laundry, peeling the vegetables, cleaning out the car, making the bed, bathing the children—keeps us all, men and women, aware of the struggles embedded in every dimension of life.

It also keeps us in touch with one another, with those we love and whose love carries us in all the small, hidden little ways we barely notice—but cannot do without.

It makes us aware of the burdens carried by those around us, in the family and the neighborhood, whose full lives we would otherwise never know.

It gives us a sense of what it means to be a full human being, rather than a foreigner in our own homes, an outlander in our own society.

That kind of shared work makes a family a family

and a community a community, rather than a mere way station or rest home for some of us—thanks to the full-time obligations of others of us to service the physical world that enables us to go on functioning.

But manual labor in today's society is no longer—for many in the West, at least—a full-time occupation. Meals come packaged now. Housecleaning is either mechanized or simplified. Industry has, in large part, given way to services, and physical labor to technology.

We live in a time, then, when the work we do is not nearly as important as knowing *why* we do it.

For the Benedictine spirit, work is not simply work. Whatever kind of work it is—professional or technical, physical or intellectual, financial or social—it is to be *good* work, work that makes the world a better, more just, more fair, and more humane place for everyone.

"Idleness is the enemy of the soul," the Rule reminds us. That insight bears pondering.

The truth is that work has a spiritual function. It is done for the sake of the soul, not for the punishment of the body or for the gratification of the ego. Good work is meant to build into us a respect for the order and beauty that the cultivation of the spiritual life demands.

Good work is a human being's contribution to the development of humankind and the fulfillment of the universe.

In fact, why we work is the very bedrock of Benedictine spirituality. It is about the bringing of the Reign of

God on earth. It is about completing the work of God in the upbuilding of the world.

Whatever the Benedictine does—mop the floor, weed the garden, fold the clothes, write the reports, plan the programs, produce the goods—becomes an act of human liturgy in praise of what it is to be alive, to redeem creation from chaos and our souls from apathy.

Work that participates in a common project of humanity frees us from total self-centeredness and makes us a prouder, more fulfilled part of the human race.

Whatever work we do—even if it does not pertain directly to the poor or the needy, the traumatized and dispossessed—it is work that gives us the means of reaching with alms the hurting places of humanity, to which our lives are grafted simply by our being alive.

Work, in Benedictine spirituality, calls for labor—manual labor, spiritual labor, and intellectual labor—that continues the co-creation of the world. In the end, they are all part of the same condition, the same scriptural mandate "to till the garden and keep it" that is at the heart of Benedictine life.

It is all to be good work, in the tradition of the great Benedictine monasteries before us that rebuilt Europe after the fall of the Roman Empire, that saved culture and preserved learning in the Middle Ages.

Monasteries of the Heart in our own time must, as virtual communities, as committed individuals, define the social labor—the peacemaking, the culture-creating, the justice-making, the community-building—by which they shall personally or corporately be known.

Work is a path toward self-fulfillment, as well. We become better at something in ourselves—more skilled, more creative, more effective—when we work. We discover that, indeed, we are good for something.

Good work is, at the same time, its own kind of asceticism. It needs no symbolic rituals or contrived penances. The very act of continuing something until we succeed at it is soul-searing, life-changing enough.

Work also puts us in solidarity with those for whom the rewards of labor are few and far between. It keeps us conscious of the burdens of the poor, of injustice to workers, of the dignity of human labor, of the glory of ongoing creation.

It makes us equal partners with the rest of the human race in this one common human endeavor to grow the globe to wholeness.

Good work is our gift to the future. It is what we leave behind—our persistence, our precision, our commitment, our fidelity to the smallest and meanest of tasks—that will change the mind of generations to come about our sacred obligation to bear our share of the holy-making enterprise that is work.

Then we shall truly be authentic witnesses to the fact that a life lived in the scriptures shapes a universal heart and rallies the global soul.

Then it will be clear that the spiritual life is not an

escape from the world, it is a commitment to share with the world the creative potential of the monastic vision of life.

A Monastery of the Heart stands as sign to the world that whatever work we do will be done with full heart and extra effort, not for our own sake alone but for the sake of the development of the entire world.

14

Co-Creation

*"Regard all utensils and goods of the monastery as
sacred vessels of the altar."*

BENEDICTINE SPIRITUALITY is a sacramental spirituality. It holds all things—the earth and all its
goods—as sacred.

In our twenty-first-century view of life—through
the lens of the Rule of Benedict—we know now in
new ways that the earth and all its fruits are not for our
exploitation, they are for our care. We are co-creators
with God of what creation has left unfinished. What has
been left in embryo is left for us to develop. What can be
developed God trusts us to bring to full potential.

But not for ourselves alone.

Co-creation, the human commitment to continue

the work of God on earth, requires us to tend the land and conserve the waters, to till the garden and protect the animals, to use the things of the earth in ways that enhance all life now—and preserve them for later generations, as well.

The human-centered view of creation is a stunted one. It fails to recognize the *oneness* of creation, the symphony of life-forms that depend on one another to bring the universe, pulsing and throbbing with life, to a wholeness that is mutual, that reflects the full face of God rather than simply our own.

The male-centered view of creation is an incomplete, an inadequate one. It fails to recognize women as equal agents in the development of creation and so ignores half the resources of creation in the decision-making process of life.

Benedictine spirituality seeks a balanced life, one in harmony with all its parts—earth, fire, air, and water, animals, plants, females, and males—all alive in the heart of God.

To allow ourselves to become digital chips in an electronic world, isolates in an interdependent universe, women and men out of touch with the life pulse of a living God—indifferent to creation, concerned only with ourselves, and still calling ourselves good—is to mistake the rituals of religion for the sanctifying dimensions of spirituality.

In a Monastery of the Heart we are called to listen to

nature as well as to one another, to hear its groans and till its gardens, to nurture its young and maintain the purity of its air, until we ourselves become the voices for life in everything everywhere.

To do that, we must become part of the liturgy of life, treating as holy everything we touch, regarding as sacred every being alive, intent on preserving the best of what is—while we use our science and technology to protect, defend, and enhance them all.

To pursue the path of Benedictine spirituality means that we will leave whatever part of the world we inhabit—its neighborhoods and nations, its oceans and preserves, its forests and its soil—in better condition than they were before we came.

Benedictines over the centuries, following the life the Rule prescribes, laid the foundation of the towns to which they brought order and organization, hospices, learning, scripture, and art, the tools of civilization, and the sustenance of the soul.

They used every human form of education and skill to bring order out of chaos, equality to the masses, and healing to the globe.

They tilled arid land and made it green. They dried the swamps and made them flower. They hired the peasants and taught them new skills.

They seeded Europe with crops that sustained entire populations, they raised the cattle that fed and clothed, they plowed the land, they distilled liquors and brewed beer that brought joy to the heart and health to the body, and they did all of that despite the plundering and pillaging that went on around them as the forces of war and domination overran and burned down one defenseless region after another.

It is not possible to live life in a Monastery of the Heart and fail to nurture the seeds of life for every living creature, every way, everywhere.

It is on the altar of creation that we celebrate our Benedictine spirituality, as our ancestors have done before us for over 1,500 years.

15

Loving Care

"Let those who are not strong have help . . ."

PATIENCE AND CARE are two pillars of Benedictine community. They hold up before our eyes, in
blinding light, in immovable form, what is to be the
nature of our presence in the world.

There is in Benedictine spirituality a deeply compas-
sionate heart—that neither glorifies the suppression of
human feelings nor denies the reality of human needs.
Nowhere is that clearer than in the attention the Rule
gives to the needs of the elderly, the sick, and the children of the monastery.

Nowhere is it more important than in a Monastery
of the Heart, which is not designed to take people out

of the arena of normal human relationships as much as it is intended to leaven them with a Benedictine view of life.

Benedictine spirituality is not the kind of religious rigor that strips the human experience of its humanity in the name of the spiritual life.

With all its regulations and recommendations, the Rule's most basic themes are the understanding of limits, the acceptance of our differences, and the expectation of mutual support.

Benedictine spirituality is not a race to win the most "spiritual points" for strict silence, or the spiritual athleticism of lengthy fasts, or even perfect attendance at prayer.

Benedictine spirituality is a community-minded game of no-one-loses.

Whatever our boundaries or barriers, we will help one another over the finishing lines of life together. We are here to enable one another to go further. We are here to learn from the insights of the other. We are here to bring all of humanity to fullness of life.

The Rule is clear about the lengths to which a Benedictine goes to sustain the elderly, to heal the sick, to support the young in the community.

"The prioress or abbot should be extremely careful," the Rule teaches, "that they suffer no neglect." Caretakers are named, special accommodations are provided, diets beyond the common fare of the monastery are given, and "the sick may take baths whenever it is advisable," Benedict says—in a time when bathing was a luxury, not a social necessity.

Suffering is not glorified in this Rule. Loving care is its norm. Children and the elderly, it declares, "should be treated with kindly consideration."

The very humanity of a Rule designed to shape a spiritual life is a fundamental spiritual message of its own. Life is not a regimen to be endured. It is an enterprise meant to be made possible, made beautiful, at every stage.

The message to the sick, on the other hand, is a spiritual discipline for us all. "Let them not by their excessive demands distress anyone who serves them. Still, the sick must be patiently borne with, because serving them leads to a greater reward."

We are, in all instances, to be patient in our requests, and caring—gentle—in our concern for others.

No amount of special asceticism can equal the amount of spiritual growth and human maturity that comes with care for others. At the same time, healthy disregard for the unceasing demands of the self is itself a sign of good mental health.

For the monastic of the heart who lives alone, Benedictine spirituality requires an outreach to those in the family, the neighborhood, the community whose needs are being neglected.

For the seeker who belongs to a Monastery of the

Heart, it calls for attention to children, regular interaction with the elderly, and care for those whose conditions limit their own participation in the community.

Whatever the situation, whatever the group, the seeker in a Monastery of the Heart is called to build community—with the entire community.

"Whose feet will the hermit wash?" St. Basil asks, and the Benedictine answers, "Everyone's."

16

Responsibility

"Let everyone receive help as the size of the community or local conditions warrant."

BENEDICTINE SPIRITUALITY is communal. It's all about living in a world of people, with other people just as burdened by the same humanity as I am, just as broken open by life, just as full of hope and the desire to live life to the hilt. Benedictinism never intends to create a world of isolates, even for the isolated. It sets out to gather the world into one great common cause of two dimensions—union with God, and global identification with all the human community.

A Monastery of the Heart, then, must be a vision of life with God at the center and people in its heart. To ignore one or the other, however good each separate element might be, is to ignore the very heartbeat, the very ebb and flow of life. Neither without the other is whole.

Nowhere is that clearer than in the Rule's continual concern for the effects of structures on people like you and I who must maintain them.

Seekers live in the midst of the world community, and so are obliged to its institutions; we are in the service of its goals and immersed in its systems and values. Which means, of course, that it is you and I who must take to it a different way of being in the world.

Over and over again, in great ways and small, Benedict calls us to treat the rest of the world with respect, with tenderness, with understanding. In large things and small, Benedictine spirituality calls us to remember the effect of our own demands on the rest of the world.

"Necessary items are to be requested and given at the proper times, so that no one may be disquieted or distressed," the Rule says.

Yet do not burden the people around you with unnecessary demands, the Rule advises. "Do not crush the bruised reed," the Rule says, even to the abbot and prioress. "Let everyone receive help as the size of the community or local conditions warrant," the Rule recommends.

Without doubt, a Benedictine community, a Monastery of the Heart, does not take as its standards the ways of corporate authority or the norms of institutional expectations. Here we are required always to put the person first. Where we are needed at any given moment is where we are meant to be. But the responsibility to carry the human community does not depend on any single person at any single time. It depends every bit as much on the attitudes and support and help of those who are being carried.

Even more shocking to contemporary culture, where we get paid by the hour, hours do not count. I am not off duty ever from the needs of others.

I am not allowed to ignore the stress and burdens of others, just because what they are doing is not my responsibility. The truly spiritual person does not live a 40-hour-a-week life. My work exists wherever I see others who are overburdened or forever overworked.

Not everyone must do everything, but everyone must do something that benefits the world as a whole. And we must do whatever we do with total commitment to both the justice and the peace of it.

We do not pose at shaping the monastic heart.

We do not posture at believing that every work is holy.

We do not pretend to see God in everything and everyone.

We are at the disposal of the human race, in whatever form or function it presents itself to us: as neighbor, as friend, as citizen, as stranger, as artist, as disciples together on the way to God.

We are each a part of the soul of the group, knowing

that what we do, or not do, may not hurt us personally but will surely affect the very future of the community.

And then each of us, we know, will also receive from the others everything we, too, need to be our best selves.

Benedictine service is not slave labor. It is the open-handed gift of those around us, who know our limits as well as their own and put their shoulders next to ours to make life good and happy, holy and heartfelt for everyone.

Benedictine spirituality is not built on a mentality of paid service for contracted hours. Nor is it built by placing unending expectations on the willing.

It is built on the trust that each of us will lay our lives down for the other, as Jesus did, and count everything we do as the privilege of participating in the co-creation of the world.

For that we pray daily, "O God, come to my assistance, O God, make haste to help me"—knowing that we, too, are at least part of everyone else's answer to that prayer.

17

Hospitality

"Once guests have been announced, meet them with all the courtesy of love."

IT IS POSSIBLE, of course, to make community out of "our kind of people," out of people who look like us and think like us and have the same backgrounds we do. But that is not the kind of life the ancient Rule has in mind or a Monastery of the Heart sets out to be.

And with good cause.

When Benedict of Nursia began his new way of living in wild, licentious, sixth-century Rome, he turned that world upside down. He took into his monastic community the rich and the poor, the slave and the free, the young and the old, artists and craftsmen, peasants and noblemen. It was a motley crew.

And then, as if that weren't enough, he opened the doors of the monastery to anyone who came, at any time, to anyone who knocked, no matter who they were or where they had been in life along the way.

Most of all, he made of their coming a royal affair.

Benedict's community met everyone with friendship and trust and honor. The pilgrim, the poor, and the stranger all became new royalty at the monastery door. "Jesus," the Rule teaches, "is to be welcomed in them."

For the sake of welcome, the daily silence was broken, the table was set, and the abbot ate with the guest.

"Great care and concern are to be shown," the Rule goes on, "in receiving poor people and pilgrims because in them more particularly Jesus is received."

The point is clear: the guest, to the Benedictine, is much more than simply another social contact. Guests, the unknown and the wandering other, are the final and authentic addition to a Benedictine life.

Without welcoming the other, the very notion of Benedictine spirituality is suspect, is nothing but more of the same. Without the guest we make our life all about us alone.

Families and communities that concentrate only on themselves do not build up the entire human family. The person with a Benedictine heart, on the other hand, is actually on the lookout for guests—for their needs, for their wisdom.

Like Abraham, whose desert tent was open on all four

sides for fear a traveler might be missed, the Benedictine heart takes special care to make itself available to the needs of the world.

"At the door of the monastery," the Rule reads, "place a sensible person."

"This porter will need a room near the entrance so that visitors will always find someone there to answer them," the Rule tells us. "As soon as anyone knocks or a poor person calls out, the porter will reply, 'Thanks be to God.'"

Thank God, you've come, Benedictine spirituality says to the stranger—to disturb our perfect lives. It's guests who refuse to allow us to become snug and secure in our little monastic hideaway.

The guest intrudes on our time and makes demands on our energy and pries open our closed minds and stretches our hearts to the breaking point. The guest refuses to allow us to see the spiritual life as an exercise in making neat and tidy schedules for ourselves. The guest saves us from counting as holiness the ironclad world of the self that we have managed to construct and structure so well.

We must never forget that guests bring us God in the guise of the immediate and the urgent, the uncomfortable and the unknown.

Most of all, perhaps, the unexpected ones, the passersby, the needy and unknown at the door expose our emptiness of heart and total self-centeredness, when we may not even know ourselves that it exists.

The guest in Benedictine spirituality is a visit from the God of Surprises who comes upon us at our most vulnerable moments and breaks us open to a new part of ourselves as well as to the needs of the other.

Guests bring the world in, place it at our feet, and dare us to be who and what we say we are. They are a blatant sign for all to see that any intent to shape a Monastery of the Heart that exists only for itself and its own kind, is really not a Monastery of the Heart at all.

A true Monastery of the Heart has stretchable, permeable, illimitable boundaries made up of anyone who happens to come into it at any time, and it accepts them, saying, "We are here for you."

OUR
PROMISE

———— •◆• ————

18

A Listening Heart

*"Listen carefully to my instructions . . . and attend
to them with the ear of your heart."*

THERE IS A MAGNET in a seeker's heart whose true
north is God. It bends toward the Voice of God
with the ear of the heart and, like sunflowers in the sun,
turns all of life toward the living of the Word.

This listening heart is pure of pride and free of arrogance.
It seeks wisdom—everywhere, at all times—and knows
wisdom by the way it echoes the call of the scriptures.

The compass for God implanted in the seeker's heart
stretches toward truth and signals the way to justice.

It is attuned to the cries of the poor and oppressed
with a timbre that allows no interruption, no smother-
ing of the Voice of God on their behalf.

These seekers hear the voice of God in the cry of the poor and oppressed, and they "immediately put aside their own concerns" and follow God's call in their actions.

Monastics cling to the Rule of Benedict in order to know a wisdom not their own, to discover the tradition on which they stand, to heed the Word of God with a steadfast heart and single-minded desire. They know that the will of God comes embedded in many shapes and forms, and that each is bringing them to the fullness of God's will for them, in mind, heart, and soul. They give themselves to the demands of life as they would to a prayer schedule itself.

In that spirit, seekers give themselves to the kind of obedience that seeks the will of God in every instance of life. They concentrate themselves on the voice of God speaking through the communal voice of the world and calling them to rise above the clamors of self-centeredness. They do the hard work of community-living and decision-making in the world around them, "not cringing or sluggish or half-hearted, but free from any grumbling or any reaction of unwillingness." And they do it so that the Reign of God can come sooner because we have been here.

In a Monastery of the Heart, Benedictine listening honors the function of discernment to point us in the direction of truth, but knows that neither dependence nor license nor authoritarianism are a valid substitute for personal discernment, for seeking truth in the light of one another's wisdom.

Discernment is a holy hearing of prophetic voices among us. It comes out of listening to others and responding to them in the name of God, so that we can move forward together, one heart at a time.

Benedictine spirituality requires careful listening and responding to the Word of God, to the call of the Jesus who leads us, and to the call of whatever community is the foundation of our spiritual life. It is not an obedience that rests on blessed ignorance, or infantile dependence, or reckless irresponsibility, or military authoritarianism, or blind submission in the name of holiness. A truly listening heart knows that we lose the chance for truth if we give another—any other—either too much, or too little, control over the conscience that is meant to be ours alone.

And yet, at the same time, personal discernment and mutual obedience—holy listening—forever seeks the spiritual dialogue holy wisdom demands. In a Monastery of the Heart, it is the acceptance of wisdom not our own that asks of us the spiritual maturity that listens first and always to the Word of God—and allows the Word to be the testing ground of every other demand made on our lives.

An authentic claim to obedience does not deny another person's independence and autonomy of thought. Discernment hones the seeker for the sake of the growth of the community and the spreading of the Word. This listening with the heart to the insights of another is not the obedience of children, or soldiers, or servants, or minions. It is the obedience given to a lover, because of love alone. It is obedience to the will of God for our lives and the good of others.

19

Conversion of Heart

"It is high time for us to arise from sleep."

EVERY LIFE IS one long list of defining moments: at one moment, we discover that what we have done with our lives to this point is not really what we are meant to do; at another moment, we come to realize that we have actually done very little with our lives at all.

At a different moment, we plot a course whose purpose is a better future—and we struggle with the thought of the energy it will take to do it.

At some moment, we suddenly recognize the fact that we have been feverishly expending energy—like walkers on a treadmill—going nowhere at all.

Or, just as bad, we become aware that we have been living good lives morally, mentally, materially, but that in the center of ourselves, in the heart of our small worlds, we can see nothing of value, nothing lasting to show for it.

We are alive, but only somewhat. We are good, but only vacantly at best. We have kept all the rules, done all the right things, said all the right prayers, but something we cannot even name, let alone define, is missing.

We find ourselves living in a spiritual shell that runs on routine, rather than the electricity of the Spirit. We are, yes—we breathe and move and seem to do—but we are not the cauldron of purpose and purity of heart we had always hoped to be.

But Benedictine spirituality reverses that.

To live in the spirit of a Monastery of the Heart is to be led daily, from one moment of prayer to the next, to the depth of the sacramental life, to the consciousness that all of life is sacred and that every act of ours makes life either more—or less—holy.

Benedictine spirituality calls us to the tasks of living, and refuses to allow anything we do to be lost to the economy of holiness: not kitchen tasks, not reading, not personal relationships, not work, not even our small service to strangers.

It confronts us with a moral determination to care for the poorest of the poor, to respect the whole of society, to open our arms to the entire gamut of life and see it as our obligation to participate in the co-creation of the world.

It steeps us in the mind of God, hour after hour, day after day, year after year, all the days of our lives.

To be a monastic of the heart prods us to see ourselves—what we think about, what we talk about, what we promote, what we ignore—as part of the character of the world, not as a bystander, not as an observer.

It creates in us the awareness that everything we do is part of Benedictine asceticism, everyone we touch is essential to our building up of the human community, every hour we spend is an anthem, an alleluia, to the work of God in us.

There is simply nothing that is unimportant in Benedictine spirituality. It is to that sense of wholeness that Benedictine sanctity aspires. It is out of that sense of oneness that Benedictine spirituality welcomes every person at the door, takes on every task to be done, listens to every voice and idea, inhales every moment of beauty that sweeps away all the dross of our souls.

Benedictine spirituality is God-with-us everywhere at every moment. The integration of all the little parts of our small lives into the one great enterprise of seeking God—who is at the heart, in the foundation, the beginning and the end of it all—is the essence of conversion of heart in a Benedictine life.

To the Benedictine, conversion of heart is the turning of the soul toward its endpoint at all times.

Conversion of heart regards nothing as "secular" or unimportant; it leaves nothing out of the equation of sanctity. It lives in a state of continual contemplation, where the face of God is as clear as lightning in the dark—because we have finally learned to see, beyond everything that is, to the mind of the God who made it.

The conversion of life that is at the basis of Benedictine holiness comes when, as a Monastery of the Heart, we finally realize that God's will for us is that we come to realize that all things are of God—all the moments of our lives, however stumbling they may be—and that all things call us to melt into one great paean of praise for the joy of having found the God we continue to seek.

20

Stability of Heart

*"Do not . . . run away from the road that
leads to salvation."*

THE WILL OF God in life does not come in straight
lines, or clear signs, or certain choices.

Life is not a set of constants to which we cling for
security or seek for affirmation. On the contrary, life is
often confusing and blurred, unsure underfoot, tentative
and shaky to the touch.

Our relationships do not feel as firmly fixed as they
once did. The work is no longer invulnerable to change.
The world around us has tilted and tipped without our
permission.

Nothing is what it once had been, nothing is what it
promised to be.

But one thing is inescapable: the way we deal with whatever happens to us on the outside will depend entirely on what we have become on the inside.

Wherever we have fixed our hearts, whatever it is to which we have given them, will determine the way we experience all that is happening to us now. Indeed, it is stability of heart, not stability of place, that is the real monastic gift.

Stability of heart—commitment to the life of the soul, faithfulness to the community, perseverance in the search for God—is the mooring that holds us fast when the night of the soul is at its deepest dark, and the noon-time sun sears the spirit.

When life seems unclear, out of control, wavering, it is stability in a Monastery of the Heart that leads us from one day to the next.

When life tastes least satisfying, it is stability of heart that continues to trust in the zest for life.

When life seems to have abandoned us, broken its promises, petered out to nothingness, it is stability of heart that reminds us that we are on our way yet to what we are meant to be—if we will only stay the course.

"Monastics may be assigned a burdensome task," the ancient Rule teaches. "If so, they should, with complete gentleness and obedience, accept the order given." Let us continue to trust that whatever the obstacles we face, whatever the walls that entrap us, whatever the spiritual fatigue that weighs us down, the God of our heart is in the midst of it, waiting for us still to make it clear.

But stability of heart in a monastery without walls, a monastery where single-mindedness and a common spirit are the foundation on which we stand, is not easy. It is not simple in its meaning or comfortable in its demands. Yet it is the promise of stability that tells us to push on when we are tired of pushing.

Stability of heart tells us that the prayer and the work and the service and the study and the reading and the believing are worth it, even when all of it has never felt more useless, more pointless, more empty of the God we had hoped to find there.

Stability is not in vogue in a world obsessed with change. This world tells us to move on when things get hard. This world tells us to start over rather than to finish what we have begun.

The culture of change tells us to fashion our worlds according to us, to refuse the struggles that come our way, to hew an easier path than one according to the Gospels—which lead us beyond the struggles of the day to the resurrection of spirit that comes in their aftermath.

The wisdom of the Rule tells us instead, "Do not be daunted immediately by fear and run away from the road that leads to salvation. It is bound to be narrow at the outset." It is a long journey, this search for God. It is constructed of patience and trust, of perseverance and persistence, of the routines of dailiness, and the cataclysmic interruptions of time.

But through it all, Benedictine spirituality knows, there is only one invariant on which we must depend: the steadiness—the stability—of the heart of God, and the constancy of knowing that "as we progress in this way of life and in faith," as the Rule assures us, "we shall run on the path of God's commandments, our hearts overflowing with the inexpressible delight of love."

OUR
SPIRITUAL
GROWTH

———— •◆• ————

21

Humility

"After ascending all these steps of humility, we will quickly arrive at the 'perfect love' of God which 'casts out fear.'"

IN BENEDICTINE SPIRITUALITY, there is a twelve-rung ladder that leads to God.

This ladder that reaches between us and God is called "the steps of humility."

The interesting thing about humility is that in the Rule—a document on spiritual development—its cornerstone principle requires the acceptance of our earthiness, the embrace of our humanity as the very stuff of our holiness. Our humanity, the Rule implies, is the clay upon which the Divine Potter and the heat of life's kiln work to shape and glaze our pliant selves into vessels of the God-life within.

Humility is the antidote to the myth of perfectionism that eats away at the heart of the spiritual life, drowning it in depression, sinking it in despair, leading us to abandon the very thought of a truly spiritual life—given the human propensity to become enmeshed in the very failures we fear.

Humility is, as well, an antidote to an achievement-driven, image-ridden, competitive society that is the hallmark of the modern age.

And yet, it is precisely who we are—with all our moral weaknesses, all our spiritual fatigue—that is the stuff of our eventual glory. The willingness to struggle with our weaknesses is, in fact, the very proof of the sincerity of our commitment to live life in a Monastery of the Heart.

It is here, in a community of seekers, sustained by their support and guided by their wisdom, that we strive ever more and more to become the fullness of ourselves fulfilled in the heart of God.

If this support and guidance are the very evidence of God's goodness to us, our ascent up the ladder of humility is the measure of our response because it is here that we become most human.

Benedict's ladder of humility begins, oddly, in surrender to an awareness of the presence of the God we seek as already within us, and it ends in personal serenity. It links, without apology, both the spiritual and the material dimensions of life and makes them one. It shows us just how tightly woven our spiritual life—and the way we live it—are meant to be.

The function of the spiritual life is not to reject our humanity but to acknowledge our neediness to bring it to fullness.

The steps on the ladder of humility are clear ones:

The first step of humility is that we "keep 'the reverence of God always before our eyes' and never forget it."

To realize the presence of God—whatever our own moral state—makes the spiritual life a companionship with God, not God a trophy to be won by perfect adherence to all the rules of life—of which we are obviously perfectly incapable.

The first step of humility dispels all notions of "merit theology." We simply do not need to "earn" God—in fact, we cannot earn God, none of us, not even the holiest among us. The truth is, Benedict teaches, we already *have* God and we must not forget it. We must simply recognize that God is God—and we are not. We are not in control; we are simply on the way to recognizing God, wherever God may be found.

Humility tells us that God is with us and within us always.

The second step of humility is "that we love not our own will . . . rather we shall imitate by our actions that saying of Jesus, 'I have come not to do my own will, but the will of the One who sent me.'"

This step of humility calls us to realize that God's will is best for us, whether we understand that will when we are faced with it or not.

Humility teaches us that the God who is good wishes me well and not woe, that I am the dust God has destined for the stars. The second step of humility says that the marrow of the spiritual life lies in learning to trust the God who created us.

The third step of humility is that, for the sake of our growth, we be willing to put ourselves under the spiritual guidance of others—not to be chained for their use, not to obey for the sake of "obeying," but for the sake of being led to the very height of our own potential, beyond our own present insights.

The third step of humility instills in us that we must be willing to receive spiritual direction.

The fourth step of humility is that if "difficult, unfavorable, or even unjust conditions" are our lot in life, that we "endure it without weakening or seeking escape," that we must learn to persevere in order to discover what darkness—as well as light—has to teach us.

Life is not a straight line, not even the spiritual life. There are obstacles and obstructions, resistance and regrets, in the path everywhere.

Humility enables us to understand that there are reasons for darkness, blessings in difficulties, hope to be gained from struggles that scour the soul of the dross of spiritual ennui. The fourth step of humility tells us to endure through the mist of life's spiritual night until the light rises once again in us.

The fifth step of humility, the Rule says, is when we "do not conceal . . . any sinful thoughts" nor "any wrongs committed in secret." This step of humility is the unmasking project of our lives. It frees us to be who we are and become who we must, despite the judgments of others.

It means that we must never allow our image—even our own image of ourselves, let alone the image of us held by those around us—to exceed the real truth about ourselves. Once we have acknowledged who we are, there is no amount of calumny that can ever really hurt us again.

The fifth step of humility says that acknowledging our faults will save us from falling victim to the false impressions that keep us in public chains to the ideas of others about us, that trap us into pretending to be who we are not.

The sixth step of humility counsels us to be "content with the lowest and most menial treatment." We foreswear the best theater tickets and car, the best house and clothes, the best table at the restaurant, and the best office in the building. We don't expect to be served. We don't expect to be made an exception. We don't expect to be preferred. It is a freeing experience, the attainment of this step of humility.

The sixth step of humility says that when we are satisfied with whatever we get, we can never be disappointed again.

The seventh step of humility is that "we not only admit with our tongues but are also convinced in our hearts that we are inferior to all and of less value."

It is at this step on the ladder of humility that we stop judging others, that we can really begin to hear the caring and insightful criticism of others, because we have finally admitted to ourselves both our highest potential and our greatest weaknesses.

Once we ourselves recognize to what depths we are capable of sliding, we stop defending ourselves from other people's criticisms of us, from others' questions about us, and we stop blaming everybody else for what *we* have surely done. Gone is the defensiveness that has cemented us in an unwillingness to change. We know ourselves now—human in every dimension, every desire, every reaction, every response—to be capable of anything and everything.

Emptier now of self, we no longer react with shock at the iniquity of another and begin to empathize instead with the fissures of soul with which they also struggle. We are no longer shocked or repulsed by the failings we see around us, because we truly know that in the same circumstances we could have, would have, done the same—or worse—ourselves.

We know who we are—and who we might have been. We are no longer so implacably certain of our own deep-down virtue.

This step of humility means that we have come to the

point where we can let go of self-righteousness, knowing that "There but for the grace of God go I."

The eighth step of humility is that "we do only what is endorsed by the common rule of the monastery."

To learn from a community does not mean that every generation does precisely what every generation before it has done, that nothing can change as time goes by, that holiness lies in the past. But it *does* mean that the constants of monastic life are not monastic practices but monastic *values*.

How commitment to prayer was practiced in the sixth century is merely history. That commitment to prayer is regular, psalm-centered, and scriptural—and continues even now—is truly Benedictine.

Peace and care for creation, concern for human community and work, discernment, prayer and prayerful reading, equality, hospitality, and conversion of heart— these are eternal Benedictine values, these are the ideals upon which the Benedictine tradition rests.

Not to learn these, not to live these, is not to be a monastic of the heart.

The eighth step of humility requires us to take our responsibility to renew the tradition in fresh new ways in every age.

The ninth step of humility is that we "control our tongues and remain silent, not speaking unless asked a question." Learning to listen to the other is every bit as much a part of humility as learning to be silent ourselves.

There is such a thing as a bitter silence, a barren silence, a busy silence that simply cuts the rest of the world out of our lives. But valuing the words of others, listening to their concerns, learning from their insights, admitting their intelligence, honoring their ideas, is the very center of human community.

These are the deepest elements in the human dialogue. Without them, no dialogue is possible, only empty, posturing, aimless words.

This ninth step of humility calls us to listen to everyone around us, to make no exceptions—and we will hear the voice of God in the world.

The tenth step of humility is that "we are not given to ready laughter, for it is written, 'Only fools raise their voices in laughter.'" Here the warning is not against enjoying ourselves, not against having fun. It is against making fun and joy impossible for everybody else.

The warning is directed at the loud and boisterous who take all the air out of the room, who make real conversation impossible, who draw all attention to themselves, who lack gravity and reflection and make it impossible for everyone else, as well.

Here humility leads us to learn what a really good time is for everyone else, and never to use ridicule of another as the counterfeit of it.

The eleventh step of humility is that "we speak gently and without laughter . . . , briefly and reasonably."

Humility requires that our conversations are never barbed or bitter, that we use no group, no community, for the sake only of the personal agendas of the self. Benedictine spirituality leads us to free ourselves from recrimination and the acid of revenge.

The eleventh step of humility says that to create a Monastery of the Heart we must speak words of peace peacefully, and words of care carefully, and words of love lovingly, and all words gently.

Finally, the twelfth step of humility teaches "that we always manifest humility in our bearing no less than in our hearts."

The humble person is not haughty, does not strut, does not shout or bully or command or impose. Rather, the humble person is simple and quiet and serene—walking and sitting, standing and talking, "or anywhere else . . . ," always aware of their own guilt and so judging no one else's.

It is, in essence, in humility—in the sense of our place in the universe—that the spiritual life must both begin and end.

Humility speaks of our relationship to God, our relationship to the spiritual teachers around us, to the development of the self beyond self-centeredness, and finally to what it means to cultivate humble relationships with others.

Humility teaches us, ultimately, that personal growth is a process, not an event, and that self-love—the narcissism that makes us the center of our own universe—is destructive of the self.

In the end, the twelve steps are simple ones. Humility leads us

(1) to recognize that God is God;

(2) to know that God's will is best for us;

(3) to be willing to receive direction;

(4) to endure and don't grow weary;

(5) to acknowledge faults;

(6) to be content with less than the best;

(7) to let go of image-making;

(8) to learn from the community;

(9) to listen to others;

(10) to abandon the urge to ridicule;

(11) to speak kindly;

(12) to be simple, to be serene.

Then Benedict makes the only promise in the entire Rule: "After ascending all these steps of humility, we will quickly arrive at the 'perfect love' of God which 'casts out fear.'"

And that is a guarantee deeply to be desired.

22

Spiritual Tools

"These are the tools of the spiritual craft."

BENEDICTINE SPIRITUALITY is clear: Beware the spirituality, the Rule implies, that lacks balance, that lacks the fullness of the spiritual life, that revolves around mystique and mystery, around esoteric ritual or secret knowledge.

Life with God at its center, as the beat of its heart, is far simpler than that.

"First of all, 'Love God with your whole heart, your whole soul and all your strength, and love your neighbor as yourself,'" Benedict says. That is the end, the purpose, and the essence of Benedictine spirituality. Everything else is practice.

The one whose life is lived in a Monastery of the Heart seeks to make Benedictine spirituality a living, vibrant part of contemporary society. Here life with God rests in steeping ourselves in the spiritual traditions that show us the fundamental path to love of God and love of humankind.

Benedict's "Tools for Good Works" lay out a way of life that is simple and clear, deeply traditional yet fully contemporary.

It rests in our becoming fully adult—in charge of our emotions and our appetites and our egotism: "You are not to act in anger . . . ," the Rule says. "Rid your heart of all deceit. Never give a hollow greeting of peace or turn away when someone needs your love." Life with God, it is clear in the teachings of Benedict, rests as much on our being humanly loving members of the human community as it does on regular repetition of revered religious exercises.

The Tools are a directory of the cornerstone documents of the spiritual life—the commandments, the corporal and the spiritual works of mercy, the steps of humility, the demands of community, the dictates of the spiritual life. They show us what it takes to develop a holy heart, to be an involved human being, a good community member, a mature person, a spiritual adult, a God-centered seeker.

"Your way of acting should be different from the world's way," Benedict directs. "The love of God must come before all else." Then everything else in life takes its proper place.

These spiritual tools call us to come to the fullness of life by coming to balance in all things. To shape in ourselves a Monastery of the Heart, then, is to avoid the kind of extremes that mask as asceticism, that play at holiness, but which, down deep, work to skew either our perspective on life or our appreciation of it.

The Tools remind us that we must not, in anything, be given to excesses that drain us of the energy for life or mire us in the kind of disinterest that distances us from the demands of life around us. Spiritual maturity, we come to see, requires us to be ardent in our search for emotional maturity—to damp down our petty little jealousies or our instinct to incite strife; to love both the young and the old; to pray for our enemies and make peace before the setting of the sun.

The Tools for Good Works are a call to us to respect tradition and, at the same time, to regard the present as the place where God waits for us to grow and create and become the best we can be in our own time. The Tools demand of us fidelity to the spiritual practices that immerse us in the presence of God. They require us to commit ourselves to peace and justice, to the poor and needy, to honesty and integrity. And, the Rule reminds us, even if we have tried and failed in all these things, tried and failed again, and tried and failed again, we must "never lose hope in God's mercy."

Benedictine spirituality is the strikingly powerful "middle way" between indifference to the spiritual life and extremism in the spiritual life.

Benedict's Tools for Good Works call each of us to be monastics of the heart in whom the commandments guide our relationship both with God and with the world in which we live. With their emphasis on the spiritual and corporal works of mercy, they call us, too, to be God-like members of the human community. "You must relieve the lot of the poor," the Rule teaches, "'clothe the naked, visit the sick,' bury the dead, help the troubled and console the sorrowing."

They remind us that to be wholly spiritual we must be wholly human. We must be humanity at its best. We must be a fully human human being, psychologically, spiritually, and emotionally mature—a human being reaching for the stars that bring us home to the One who made us more than the clay we've been given to shape on our way.

23

Sacred Art

"They are to practice their craft with all humility."

THE BOND BETWEEN Benedictine spirituality and art goes deep. Medieval monasteries were centers of the arts and patrons of the arts because art, as a reflection of beauty—which is itself an attribute of God—came to be understood, in theological terms, as simply another sign of the living presence of God.

Sacred images, music, and architecture transcend the distractions of matter. Art gives both consciousness and expression to the presence of God in time. Art, monastics of every century knew, gives us new ways to see the unseeable. Soaring spires, awesome cloisters, and grand chapterhouses became hallmarks in ages past of monastic life.

In our own age, paintings and illuminations, grand music and great poetry, deep and honest writing, and the sculpting of the spiritual in human form all speak of the mystical dimensions of monastic life, still come out of spirits thirsty for God. The beauty of creation, of God, monastics reasoned, is of the essence of life. There is a responsibility to nurture it.

No wonder that artists of all ilk flocked to monasteries across Europe, to make visible the infinite dimensions of the invisible God and work there yet in its pursuit. Clearly, the artist and the monastic seek the same thing. They are embarked on the same journey. They are devoted to the same end. They both believe that spirit is greater than matter, but that matter is its borning place.

Monasteries and monastic churches have always drawn artists like magnets attract steel.

A Monastery of the Heart, then, cannot leave the world or any place in it called Benedictine—our homes, our work places, our prayer and reflection areas—to the deterioration and disorder that comes from the soul that is unattuned to the beauty of God, reflected in the beauty of creation.

Monasticism exists in pursuit of the beauty of the invisible God. Art makes shining slivers of that beauty visible. To develop the soul is to develop the essence of an artist.

Monasticism is the one path of life that declares itself to be the single-minded search for God in life—before which all other pursuits pale. It is an exercise in living every day on a plane above itself, of seeing in the obvious more than the obvious, in finding even in the mundane the creative energy that drives human creation to heights that end in bursts of beauty—in the self and in the world around it. If, indeed, truth is beauty and beauty truth, then the monastic and the artist are one.

Basic to monasticism are the very qualities art demands of the artist: silence and contemplation, discernment of spirit and humility. Basic to art are the very qualities demanded of the monastic: single-mindedness, the search for beauty, immersion in praise and creativity. The meaning of one for the other makes for both great art and greatness of soul.

It is a love for human community that puts the eye of the artist in the service of truth. Knowing the spiritual squalor to which the pursuit of anything less than beauty can lead us, the artist lives to stretch our senses beyond the tendency to settle for lesser things—simplistic stories instead of great literature, bland characters rather than great portraits, tasteless decorations instead of artistic accessories, plastic flowerpots instead of pottery.

Finally, it is humility that enables an artist to risk rejection and failure, disdain and derogation, to bring to the heart of the world what the world too easily, too randomly, too callously overlooks.

In Benedictine spirituality, we are all formed in the monastic art of the search of ultimate Beauty. Clearly, great art is a very spiritual thing. More, a great spiritual life is itself a piece of great art. It is the ultimate creativity. It is an external sign of the interior artistry of a Monastery of the Heart to create such beauty, and then to give its beauty away as freely and as recklessly as possible, so that every human soul can see in it another, a better, image of God.

It is one of the great gifts of Benedictine spirituality that a Monastery of the Heart can give: that we spend ourselves making the world as beautiful as God, the Artist, the Word, meant it to be.

24

Good Zeal

*"Just as there is a wicked zeal of bitterness which
separates from God, so there is a good zeal
which leads to God."*

THE RULE OF Benedict was written in the sixth century, in an ascetical climate more given to personal
self-denial than to the discipline of community building.
If there is any segment of this Rule, however, that speaks
to its humanity, its soul, its basic approach to the spiritual
life, it is the chapter on "The Good Zeal of Monastics."

Rather than calling for strict adherence to personal
disciplines, the chapter makes an important distinction
between "evil—distorted—zeal" and "good zeal." It is
an important spiritual reflection for all of us who set out
to form a Monastery of the Heart, where most efforts at

the spiritual life are private and personal, unmonitored and undefined, and so always subject to being either too extreme a reaction or too little a response. If there is a temptation in the spiritual life, it is, as the Rule makes clear, "to aspire to be called holy before you really are."

It is the temptation to measure ourselves—and others —according to the norms laid down by a distorted zeal, a neurotic religiosity that gets satisfaction out of extremes and calls them "the spiritual life." Distorted zeal rests for its confirmation on a series of private exercises designed to test the spiritual athleticism of the human spirit; it calls for rigorous adherence to personal practices designed to wear down the body in order to damp the impulses of the soul.

Spiritual practices of this sort call for harsh fasts and long prayer periods, for intense regimes of self-denial and withdrawal, all of which are sincere, certainly, and all of which are signs of commitment to the spiritual life. But at the same time, all of these practices can be mistaken for the very thing they seek: the conversion of heart that attunes a person to the will of God for the world.

Worse, those who practice this kind of distorted zeal, make themselves the measure by which they evaluate and determine the spiritual life of others, as well. Drained of mercy and sapped of spirit, they lose contact with the very God of love for whom, they say, they search.

The criteria for the good zeal which the Rule of Benedict makes the standard of Benedictine spirituality, on the other hand, is that it must be practiced "with fervent love." The qualities of good zeal, as the ancient Rule describes them, are almost too simple for souls more interested in keeping spiritual score than in living a spiritual life:

We must be zealously devoted to one another—in such a way that we give preference to the needs and wishes of the other.

We must bear with zealous patience the infirmities, "whether of body or mind," of those around us.

We must zealously compete with one another only in our attempt to listen well to the wisdom and needs of others, rather than to center only on our own.

We must zealously do what is best for others, rather than concentrate simply on what we have decided is best for ourselves.

We must zealously love one another chastely and appropriately, not selfishly or exploitatively.

We must be in zealous awe of the presence of God in us and around us.

We must zealously love our community, its tradition and its teachers, with real affection.

Most of all, we must prefer nothing in the world to the love of God.

Then, if we do these things—if we bring to the world a Monastery of the Heart—with this kind of zeal, we will have reached the heights of love to which Benedictine spirituality is designed to bring us.

25

Peace

"Turn away from evil and do good; let peace be
your quest and aim."

OVER THE ARCHWAY of medieval monasteries were
commonly carved the words *Pax Intrantibus*—
"Peace to those who enter here." These words were
both a hope and a promise.

Benedict's vision of the peaceable kingdom was a real
one. In a society struggling with social chaos, awash in
the evils of classism, prey to foreign encroachment on
all sides—and at the mercy of wave after wave of war-
ring forces, highway piracy, and the widespread social
disorganization and moral deterioration that came with
the fall of the superpower Rome—Benedict sketched
out a blueprint for world peace. He laid a foundation

for a new way of life, the ripples of which stretched far beyond the first monastery gates to every culture and continent, from one generation to another, from that era to this one, from his time and now to ours. To us. To you and me.

Peace is our legacy, our mandate, our mission, as alive today as ever, more in need today—in a nuclear world, a world of starving peoples—than ever. Benedictine peace, however, is not simply the absence of war. It is a lifestyle that makes war unacceptable and violence unnecessary. It is not a lifestyle dominated by control and a plethora of rules. It is a lifestyle that foregoes violence on every level, for any reason.

Most of all, this lifestyle is a simple one. It is basic in its elements, not difficult to achieve, simple to sustain. It nurtures neither ambition nor greed. It is straightforward in its values, without being either esoteric or convoluted.

These values are clear ones: the development of sound human communities, of prayer, stewardship, equality, stability, conversion, peace—all designed to make for lights of love shining in a world given to violence. It is a lifestyle committed to its ideals before all else, and intent on opening its arms and taking the world into its Monastery of the Heart.

It is, then, an oasis of human peace in a striving, searing, simmering world.

Benedictine spirituality is a counterculture that calls for a rhythm of life that honors and enables, stretches and challenges, every dimension of human development. It creates community out of a collection of strangers—a slice of life that crosses age levels, economic backgrounds, and ethnicities—to where differences can be honored, and differences can be broached, and peace can come to both the person and to an entire population at the same time.

Benedictine spirituality is a life that honors the earth and cultivates the planet for the sake of all the people of the earth. It is a holy life. It passes on to the next generation a society and a globe that is in better condition than it was—because people with a Benedictine heart have taken their responsibility to protect it for the future.

It allows no waste but provides for the needs of all. It allows no class distinctions but thrives on the differences that the human condition demands. It aims for the highest standards of personal behavior and, at the same time, understands and supports those for whom growth is a struggle and the social standards of life seem always to be a work in progress.

Finally, Benedictine spirituality requires of us all the humility that allows us no room to make gods of ourselves, to impose ourselves on the rest of the universe, to develop the hubris that leads to the oppression of others, that justifies force as the sign of our superiority, that enthrones the arrogance in us over the holiness and wholeness of others, that smothers the awareness in a person of their small and proper place in the universe.

It is humility that makes us happy with what we have, willing to have less, kind to all, simple in our bearing, and serene within ourselves. It teaches us that they who have themselves for God have a very small god indeed.

Benedictine spirituality is a recipe for peace and a prescription for a life lived well on every level.

And now, our Monastery of the Heart is ours to shape and to preserve, to share and to promote, to model and to make real in our own time.

Pax Intrantibus. Peace to those who enter here.

Epilogue

"As we progress in this way of life and in faith,
we shall run on the path of God's commandments,
our hearts overflowing with the inexpressible
delight of love."

Benedictine spirituality is not a spiritual practice that waxes and wanes, comes and goes, as we grow and change and mature in the spiritual life.

It is a way of life, a free-standing and stable model of the God-seeking human enterprise that is based on age-old traditions and ancient wisdom.

Nor is it a goal unto itself. It is, as the Rule says so directly and simply, "written for beginners."

This is the life that introduces us to a lifestyle, not to a set of prayer practices or even any defined ministry.

It is not a work that can be accomplished in any given period and then forgotten. It is the work of a lifetime.

It roots us in the scriptures and prayer.

It immerses us in the work of co-creation.

It stresses justice as the way to peace.

It does away with classism, racism, sexism, and ethno-centrism.

It sees differences as the enrichment of any community, rather than a threat to society.

It urges us to immersion in the Word of God, respect for study and reflection, and regularity at prayer.

And yet, Benedictine spirituality calls for "nothing harsh, nothing burdensome."

It leaves to each of us, as individuals and groups, the task of determining in every kind of community, of every era, what is necessary to fulfill these values and attain the riches of this life.

It calls us always to the *more* of life: to more peace, more humility, more serenity, more study, more prayer, more openness, more service of the other, more community of heart, more richness of soul, more immersion in the tradition and the wisdom it has handed on to us.

It invites us to come to learn, too, how less is also more: how less competition means more peace, less jealousy means more contentment, less need for things means more satisfaction, less self-centeredness means more happiness, and less corrosive personal ambition leaves more room for the loving presence of God.

This is a Rule, a spirituality, a lifestyle in which up is down, and low is high, and nothing is everything.

Welcome to the joys that come to the spirit the less we plague the soul with things.

Welcome to the real riches that life has to offer.

To those seekers who find in their souls a Monastery of the Heart, the possibility of happiness is unbounded, the promise of fulfillment is eternal.

Appendix

A Reader's Version of the Rule of Saint Benedict in Inclusive Language: The Chapters

Monasteries of the Heart is a movement of seekers interested in becoming part of a community of seekers, either online or with others of their own choosing, who form to support one another in shaping their spiritual lives around Benedictine values and priorities. www.monasteriesoftheheart.org